Debt-Free

9 Step System to Get Out of Debt Fast and Have Financial Freedom: The Quickest Way to Get Out of Debt Forever

by Ashton Jude

DARE TO DESIGN YOUR LIFE

THE BIG
VENTURE

Table of Contents

Who is this book for?

Do you have debt that you just *want* to get rid of more than anything?

Are you looking forward to the day you feel completely financially free?

Does the thought of having NO DEBT make you excited?

Then this book is for you!

I am going to reveal to you're the *ONLY* system that will allow you to pay off your debt at the FASTEST rate possible!

You can apply this system to ANY debt because it will increase the speed at which you pay off your debts.

These debts can include anything, such as credit card debt, car loans, personal loans, student loans, family loans, and so forth.

What will this book teach you?

I have never seen anyone outline a debt repayment system like mine. I'm not saying it doesn't already exist, but I've personally never seen it.

I have uniquely identified multiple strategies and techniques and structured them into a system that will allow you the greatest results in paying off your debt.

My system is a simple 9-step financial system that WORKS! It's been proven for years, but never taught to you.

We don't learn about money or debt at school, but I'm going to give you an education in this book that you will use for the rest of your life!

YES! This 9-step system really is that valuable!

I would like to congratulate you for downloading this book, and I encourage you to not only read it, but also take action and apply the steps I teach you into your life!

Once you start applying them, you will see the fantastic results!

Step 1 – Stop Digging!

I'm sure you're very excited to get stuck into this book and learn how you can apply this system to get out of debt in one of the quickest ways possible, however, to achieve this goal effectively there are certain things you must do first!

Stop Accumulating Debt Starting NOW!

This book is about ending bad financial habits and replacing them with good financial habits.

You've been digging a fatal hole of debt for yourself for however long those credit cards (or whatever it is) have been abused and it's now time to stop. For this system to work, no more debt can be accumulated!

If this means you have to cut your credit cards, then cut them!

If this means you have to freeze your credit cards, then freeze them!

Do whatever it takes so that you stop getting into more debt from this point forward.

From now on, whenever you are making purchases or paying bills, you do it with cash or a debit card (for those that don't know, a debit card is a card that lets you access money directly from your bank account and many banks work with the major card providers, Visa and MasterCard – therefore, a debit card can give you identical accessibility as a credit card, without the surcharges).

Get Educated on Debt

Since the majority of this book is about educating you with a system that you can apply to deal with and eliminate your debt, I can only provide a basic education on debt here.

I definitely recommend reading some further articles on debt to enhance your knowledge, however, the basics that you should know are below.

Debt relies strongly on the fact that we live busy lives and can get easily distracted. When we're distracted, debt can go undetected and we never really realize the situation we're actually in until it becomes a bit too late.

It's a way for us to make a problem go away from the present moment, thinking that we can worry about it later.

But the truth is that it will never go away; debt just becomes a bigger and bigger worry the longer it stays in our lives.

The thing is that it's so common today that most people don't even realize it's a problem in the first place, so when they are struggling with payments later in their lives it can scare them!

I personally believe that there is a lack of financial education at schools, not just in the US but also around the world (definitely in Australia – where I grew up and went to school).

We don't really learn much about money, specifically about debt, interest rates, bank accounts, financial instruments, saving for retirement, etc.

These are things that affect everyone at some point in their lives. Even if you have never had a credit card in your life and never get a home loan to buy a house, you still need some basic financial education because you have to put your money somewhere, and you also have to invest for your retirement.

Anyway, the point here is that debt relies on all of this and unfortunately it can really hurt us financially – which has the potential to lead into further problems like losing your house, your relationships, your job, and possibly leaving us with no other option except for bankruptcy. Something this powerful, I believe, should be taught to us at school!

Nevertheless, I congratulate you for reading this book now because I'm about to educate you like you've never been educated before. You're going to learn things you can apply to your life immediately. And best of all, you're going to start saying goodbye to debt forever!

Other Books By Ashton Jude

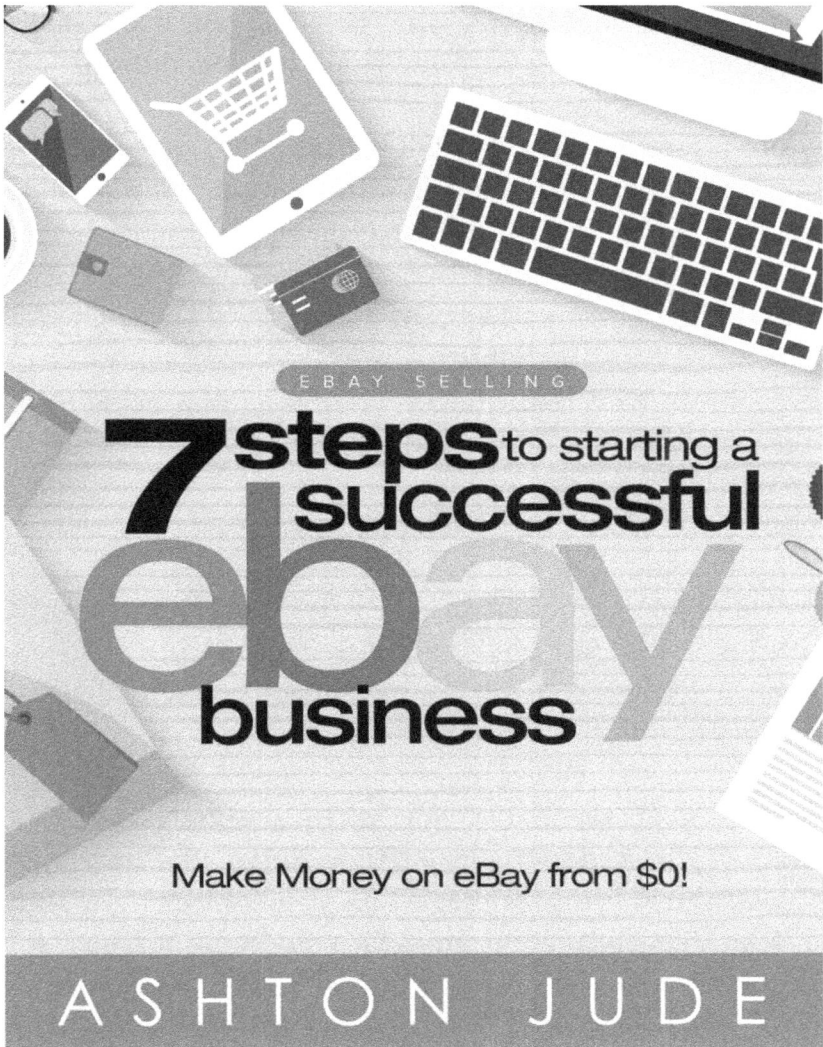

Check out: 7 Steps to Starting a Successful eBay Business

Step 2 – Let's Get Focused

Now that we've stopped the problem of accumulating more debt, we need to start focusing on the solution.

Despite a lack of financial education being one factor that can contribute to drowning in debt, another important one to acknowledge is definitely bad financial habits.

Identifying Bad Financial Habits

The problem with bad financial habits is that because they differ for everyone, most people don't even know if they have one.

The truth is that if you aren't following parts of this system I'm sharing with you, specifically the budgeting, recording and transacting parts, whether you're in debt or not, you are more likely than not to have bad financial habits to some extent.

I know that many people can get by without a budget, or without tracking down every single dollar that they spend, but what I also know is that when you start using a budget and start tracking your money, you begin to see some unnecessary expenses, or as I like to call it, "lost money".

These expenses can then be eliminated and the same money can be invested for your future, allowing you to have an earlier or more comfortable retirement, or they can be invested in a new hobby, or even an extra few days of vacation every year!

So, although you may not be able to identify any bad financial habits right now, you soon will see what they are in your life once you start applying this system.

Changing Bad Financial Habits into Good Ones

The process of changing your financial habits is exactly the same as the process of changing any other habits in your life.

Unfortunately, that also means that the high failure rate of habit changes in other parts of your life also apply to financial habits.

Now, I'm not saying you aren't very good at changing bad habits into good ones – but I am saying that *as humans,* generally speaking, we aren't very good at changing habits at all.

Think back to the times you've said you're going to *stop* doing something, only to find that after a few days or even weeks later you find yourself doing it once again (think fast food, soda, shopping, smoking, gambling, drinking, etc.).

Now think back to how many times you've said you're going to *start* doing something, only to find that after a few days or even weeks later you find yourself stopping (think working out or going to the gym, eating healthy, etc.).

It's unfortunate, but it's true. In fact, approximately a whopping 92% of people DON'T achieve the New Year's Resolutions that they set themselves every year.

So, it's not a bad assumption to make that, in general, we aren't very good at changing our habits.

There is a solution though!

To effectively change bad habits into good ones, you need to understand how humans work. You need to understand what motivates us as humans.

And then also go a step deeper and ask yourself what motivates you as a person.

As humans, we generally make decisions based on gaining pleasure or avoiding pain.

As an individual, you may make decisions based on what puts you financially ahead, what's best for your family, whether something will allow you to achieve your dreams, or maybe even whatever option is the easiest.

Whatever the case may be, I want you to sit down with a pen and piece of paper and do the following activity.

I want you to think back to one of the biggest challenges you've overcome in your life, one of your biggest accomplishments, or one of your biggest changes in habits that you have made.

Once you have one in your mind, I want you to write down on the piece of paper some of the major factors that allowed you to experience success. They may be characteristics, small habits, or a particular mindset. Whatever the case may be, write it down.

What you should have in front of you once you have done this activity is a list of the factors that you believe allowed you to experience success in the past.

These same factors can be harnessed and used to help you accelerate your success to achieving financial freedom without any debt!

I also did this activity just now, and here are my results:

Accomplishment:

Earning $32,000 in the span of six months (goal of $30,000), while attending university as a full-time student. I received an acceptance letter as an exchange student in the US exactly six months prior to my starting date, but I had nowhere near enough funds to study abroad for one year (it was a two-semester program). So, I had to put my head down, work hard, and I finally achieved it three weeks before my departure date, and had an extra $2,000 more than my goal amount.

Factors that contributed to my success:

- I broke my entire goal down into monthly goals, and then into weekly goals. This allowed me to work towards my weekly goals, so I didn't get overwhelmed thinking about my major goal (it was easier to aim for $1,200 a week than $30,000 in total).

- I thought about and researched ways that would allow me to achieve my goal – for example, I identified several methods that could achieve the income I desired once combined, and also identified several methods that could not help me (due to time constraints) and completely ignored them.

- I managed my time effectively, using to-do lists and a diary. This allowed me to still get good grades at university while working two jobs and <u>running a side eBay business</u>.

- I focused on my goal every day (had my acceptance letter stuck on my wall near my bed), particularly when I felt like I was "burned out" or "lazy". This was particularly important because around the mid-point I started feeling lazy, but remained focused on my end goal and realized how close I really was.

- Sometimes when I was bored at work, or felt myself procrastinating, I would just close my eyes and just imagine myself at college in the US. This also helped motivating me when I most needed it.

- I changed my environment to make my goal more achievable. I did this by structuring my desk, my actual laptop screen and folders, and my storage room for my stock that I sold on eBay.

Using my list as an example, I can now see where my strengths lie and structure any new goals or habit changes in the same format as this previous successful one I had, hopefully succeeding once again.

The main purpose of you doing this activity is to see that it's firstly possible for you to make positive habitual changes, and secondly, so you can actually use some personal motivators or personal methods (that worked before) to help you in your journey to becoming debt free, since it's going to be requiring goal setting, habitual changes, and effort!

Step 3 – Time to Organize Your Debt

This step is pretty simple, but it's required because it's going to give us a starting point and help us figure out what exactly we are tackling.

Put It All in Front of You

Get a piece of paper and a pen out once again. Now, here's what I want you to do when you organize your debt

1) List in Terms of Interest Rates

List your debts from the highest interest rates at the top, to the lowest interest rates at the bottom. Just keep the list simple; only include the name of the debt, or what it's for, and the dollar amount, along with the interest rate.

2) Assign an Emotional Impact Rating

Once you have the entire list of all your debts on paper, or just the one massive debt, I want you to assign a rating next to it out of 10 that rates it in terms of your emotional connection to it.

A rating of 10 means that you cannot sleep at night because it bothers you, and a rating of 1 means that you don't even care that you owe that money.

For example, if you have three loans, a student loan, a family loan and a credit card debt, you may assign a rating of 8 to the credit card debt because the interest is a whopping 20%, you may assign a rating of 5 to the student loan because the interest is less but still there, and you may assign a rating of 2 to the family loan because your parents gave you that money and they told you that you can take your time with paying it back.

The point is that this emotional rating should incorporate your feelings (frustrations or annoyance of having the loan) as well as your potential happiness and how you would feel once it's paid off.

3) Reorder Considering Interest Rate + Emotional Impact

Now, on a new section of the paper that is blank, or on a completely new piece of paper, I want you to REORDER and REWRITE that list of debt again.

This time I want you to not just rank it in terms of the interest rate, but also consider your emotional rating. The reason for this is because sometimes the emotional impact of having a certain debt is so great on our lives that we must aim to pay those off first. So, if you have any 9s or 10s for emotions, try to shuffle those high up on your list.

Obviously, if you have any insanely high interest rate loans, such as credit card debt or personal loans (especially if it's 20% or more), you need to also consider putting those at the top.

4) We Have A "Debt Sheet"

Once you have this list written, it's going to be used as your "Debt Sheet". It will tell you what debt you need to pay off next, prioritizing it in terms of potential losses (the interest rates) and emotional impacts (the emotional ratings you gave the loans).

The loan that is on the top of the list will always be the one we are targeting at any given time, once its paid off, we cross it off, and then go for the next one down.

One thing to note before we move on is that if you have the opportunity to transfer your debt all into one loan, or even transfer a few of the smaller loans together into a bigger loan, I do recommend it IF YOU ARE NOT suffering any additional losses from fees by doing it.

In Australia, there are several companies and banks that will allow you to consolidate certain credit card loans, and sometimes car loans with home mortgages, and they can be done without fees. In some cases, you can actually get a better interest rate!

That being said, there are also some institutions that allow it without fees, but then charge fees if the new loan doesn't have a certain amount paid off it within the first 90 days.

So, do your research and talk to creditors about any options they provide. If nothing can be improved, don't worry, leave things as they are and since you're surviving financially with your current debt, nothing will get worse, instead, by using this system things *will get better!*

Step 4 – What Happens to Your Money?

This step is all about assessing your current income and current expenses on a monthly basis.

Yet again, I want you to get out another piece of paper and pen. And if you're not already, get used to it. This system emphasizes accountability, and accountability is most accurate when everything is recorded!

1) Assess Your Income

I want you to write down all your expected income on a monthly basis. Look at paychecks or bank transfers from your employee/s if you have to. Consider all working income, any interest, dividends or royalties, and any other forms of income that you have.

If your income fluctuates, I want you to go to your previous six to 12 months and average out your monthly income. The point here is to create an income figure that is somewhat consistent every month.

If you get paid monthly this will be quite easy, if it's weekly or biweekly then just multiply it accordingly to get a figure for the month.

If you are in a relationship and do your finances with your significant other, then consider both your income and theirs, creating a combined income for your household.

Once you've done this, you will know you're done ONLY when you can accurately say that on your piece of paper you see EVERY possible dollar that you can expect to receive on a monthly basis.

2) Assess Your Expenses

Now I want you to write down all your expenses on a monthly basis. Again, look back at utility bills, transport costs, fuel receipts, mortgage payments, grocery bills, rent, bank fees, etc.

So, firstly you need to include every single expense that you incur on a monthly basis (things such as cable bills, telephone bills, internet bills, rent, mortgage payments, debt payments, etc.). These are the easiest because they are usually the same cost every month.

Then you need to estimate your monthly costs on things that aren't the same every month. For example, grocery bills, fuel costs, etc. For these, make sure you look at several months' worth of costs and try to average out the most accurate estimate of your monthly expenses.

One thing to note is that any expenses relating to debt (car repayments, credit card repayments, student loan repayments, mortgage repayments, etc.) are INCLUDED as expenses in this section.

Similarly to the income, you will know you are done ONLY when your paper accurately shows EVERY possible dollar you can expect to pay on a monthly basis as an expense.

3) Let's Make Some WIPE OUT MONEY!

At this point you should have an accurate outline of all your monthly income and monthly expenses. Therefore, if you compare the two you can see your overall current financial standing.

Hopefully, for your sake, your income is greater than your expenses, however, if it's the other way around then we have a lot of work to do!

The odds are that your income should at least cover your expenses, and for most people income will be slightly more than expenses.

If it weren't this way then you would be in an endless cycle that required the accumulation of new debt to pay off old debt, hence spiraling out of control. If you're at this point you would definitely be aware of it and I'd assume you would be seeking professional advice immediately.

Also, if your income is equal to your expenses, or less than your expenses, you can use the advice I give in the next two steps of this system to INCREASE your income and DECREASE your expenses so that your income will be greater than your expenses.

Anyway, assuming that your income is indeed greater than your expenses, you can now subtract your expenses from your income. This amount leftover is what I like to call your "Wipe Out Money".

Wipe Out Money is the SECRET to this system and by applying it in the most effective way to your debt (which is outlined in the rest of this book), your debt will be paid off in the quickest way possible!

4) Wipe Out Money Formula

If you haven't already figured it out, your goal is to achieve the most Wipe Out Money you can every month, because it is this money that will directly slash your debt every single month and eventually cause a massive avalanche in debt reduction for yourself.

To learn how to increase your amount of Wipe Out Money, you need to first understand how it's calculated – it's actually incredibly simple.

WOM = Monthly Income – Monthly Expenses

Simple!

So, using the above formula, to increase the amount of Wipe Out Money you have every month, you need to do one of two things:

1. *Increase* the amount of monthly income you receive.

2. *Decrease* the amount of monthly expenses you incur.

The next two steps in this system will outline many ways in which you can do both – so you can have the most Wipe Out Money possible every single month!

Remember, this system works great if you follow it properly and apply every step. The next two steps will involve you putting in a lot of effort and making several changes in your life.

Step 5 (Increasing Your Income) will require you to put in effort to earn more money every month, and I will give you several methods in doing so.

Step 6 (Decreasing Your Expenses) will require you to put in effort and more importantly, discipline, to cut down on expenses every month, and I will show you several methods and ways you can do that too!

Step 5 – Increasing Your Income

There are many ways to increase your income and, in turn, increase your Wipe Out Money, but below are some of the methods I recommend!

Some can be done as immediately as today, and others may take a few weeks to a few months. Have a read of them all and see which ones you can apply to your situation.

1) Sell Things You Don't Need, Use or Want Anymore

I highly recommend this being the first thing you do to boost your Wipe Out Money.

By selling things around your house, the first thing you should note is that it obviously won't cause a consistent increase in your income every month. That being said, it will definitely give you a nice initial boost to get the ball rolling.

Also, if you have big ticket items or toys, you should highly consider it because now is a time to focus more on eliminating your debt, rather than accumulating unnecessarily expensive big-ticket items, such as cars, boats, snowmobiles, bikes, etc.

The best part about this is you can use this as an opportunity to clean out and de-clutter your house. If this is the way you would like to go, then here's what I recommend:

- Firstly, do one room at a time in your house, and split the room up into four sections (each corner is how I like to do it).

- Secondly, take everything out of that space in the room – absolutely everything! You're essentially starting from scratch. Take it all out from that "section" and move it either into another "section" or into another room.

- Thirdly, go to all those items you removed, and ONLY bring back the things you *REALLY NEED*. Remember, you're in debt; you want to pay it off and if you don't *really need* something then you need to consider your options (listed below).

- If you have decided that you don't need the item anymore, you have three options:

  1) Sell it on eBay, Craigslist, Gumtree (for those in the UK or Australia), in a garage sale, etc.

  2) Donate it to a charity or a thrift store.

  3) Throw it out, only if it can't be sold or is of no use to anyone.

Using this strategy, you will benefit in many ways. Firstly, you will make a bunch of money from things you no longer want or need. Secondly, you will hopefully be giving a lot of items to a good cause. And finally, you will have a cleaner home.

I should also mention that when you live minimally, your expenses could be reduced (more on that in Step 6).

One last thing to mention is that you would be surprised how many valuable things are in your house right now that you can sell on eBay.

In my book, <u>7 Steps to Starting a Successful eBay Business from $0</u>, I reveal how you can go from $0 to $500+ by just selling things from around your house. I even go through each room in your house and outline the most valuable items that you are most likely not using anymore!

2) Get Another Job

The next easiest and most effective way to increase your income is to get another job.

Whether this extra job is part-time or full-time depends on your current circumstances, but it's definitely something that can increase your income and speed up your entire process to becoming debt-free.

Remember that this doesn't have to be a permanent solution, you can do it in the beginning to get the Wipe Out Money Avalanche started (more on this later in the book) and once things start moving you can reduce your hours and eventually quit this extra job.

However, if you are in a fair amount of debt or want to get rid of your debt fast, this is something I highly recommend.

3) Start Freelancing

Freelancing is basically turning your current skills into extra income. You can get paid either hourly or per project you work on, and you can work doing just about anything.

The most common jobs you can get as a freelancer includes writing, translating, transcribing, graphic designing, web designing, marketing and advertising consulting and IT consulting.

That being said, the truth is you really can work doing just about anything.

To start freelancing, go to the following websites and browse through current projects/jobs on offer:

- oDesk

- Elance

- Freelancer

- Guru

- iFreelance

- PeoplePerHour

- GetACoder

- Fiverr

I've also included Fiverr in that list, which is a website that allows you to do nearly anything for someone else for $5. Definitely check it out!

I highly recommend you take a look at all of those sites, browse through open projects, look through current openings and see if there's anything you can do.

If you find something good, it's as simple as making an account (which is free) and then bidding or applying for the project.

If you get the job, you do the work, and you get paid!

I have successfully made several thousand dollars online myself, freelancing as a writer. I started on Elance and now I have enough clients that I just have my own website up – TBVWriting.

The point is that it's possible, and I'm not just preaching without experience. Go into those sites, look at the projects and put in some effort – you will only get out what you put in when it comes to freelancing!

4) Start Up a Small Side Business

This is more so for those who aren't as skilled technologically (so they cannot get into freelancing as easily), but are more than willing to offer some "real life" services.

You can do many things for other people in your neighborhood or city and get paid for them.

Some ideas include pet sitting, lawn mowing, house cleaning, tutoring, cooking/catering, handyman work, etc.

The point here is again that you have to hustle. Put ads in your local papers, talk to everyone you know in your neighborhood, your family, your friends, local small businesses and shops, everyone – and tell them all about your new services!

5) Start an Online Business/eBay Business

There are many ways you can make money online through your own online business, and below I'm going to mention a few:

- You can start doing affiliate marketing through your own website or blog. It's essentially helping sell another person's product, and because you do that, they give you a percentage of all sales as a commission. Amazon is one of the biggest websites you can become an affiliate partner with. If this is something that sounds appealing to you, then I highly recommend you researching into it more – unfortunately, as much as I would like to discuss it in this book, teaching affiliate marketing would take up a whole book itself!

- You can create your own informational product, such as a Kindle eBook, or even just an online course about something you know. Again, you can sell this through your own website or using merchants such as Amazon. As with affiliate marketing, you will have to research more information about "creating information products" and learn about it in your own time. Maybe sometime in the near future I'll create a book about how you can do that too!

- Finally, and probably the one option I'd recommend over both affiliate marketing and informational products, is starting your own eBay business. The reason I recommend this over the others is because you can start seeing profit much quicker. I know this because I have successfully made a lot of money on eBay myself, running several eBay stores. I've written all about this in my book, <u>7 Steps to Starting A Successful eBay Business from $0</u>, and I go through step-by-step how you can start your very own eBay business by investing NO MONEY in the beginning. If this is something you're interested in, I highly recommend checking out my other book, and remember if you have any questions, you're always more than welcome to contact me via my blog – <u>TheBigVenture</u>.

6) Ask for A Promotion

One final option that you may be able to do, depending on your situation, is to ask for a promotion.

This obviously depends on how long you have been working at company for, and your current position in the company, however it's definitely something I thought I would add in because it may apply to you!

Step 6 – Decreasing Your Expenses

Below are some of my favorite ways to decrease your expenses so you can increase the amount of Wipe Out Money you have!

1) Selling Things!

Just like it's recommended to increase your income, selling things is also recommended to decrease your expenses.

Why?

Because there are many things in your life that you currently have that cost simply to maintain them. Things such as your car or TV, for example, both cost money to maintain them (fuel, insurance, and registration for your car – and cable or Netflix for your TV).

There may be many other things as well that cost money to maintain them, so definitely consider selling them or at least getting rid of them while you're on your journey to clearing your debt!

2) New Methods of Transport

Definitely consider other methods of transport that could be cheaper for you.

If you regularly drive a car, fuel is probably going to be a big expense for you. Can you carpool?

Consider walking more, taking public transport, or even riding a bicycle as much as you can. This will all reduce your expenses.

3) Cut Out the Crap!

I'm more than certain that if you're in debt you probably have a bunch of crap you don't need any more in your life.

Now, I'm not talking about all those unnecessary items you own (those should get sold to increase your income!), but I'm talking about recurring bills you're paying for crap you don't need.

You're in debt; right now, you need to consider if you really need internet in your house if you can get it for free at a local library, you need to consider if you really need to be paying for cable and/or Netflix subscriptions (or even be keeping your TV for that matter!), and definitely consider cutting out excess phone connections or cell plans.

I'm not recommending that you live like a boring person, but I'm strongly recommending you consider your current situation and how big your debt is.

You will know if I'm talking to you when I make the above recommendation – it's dependent on your situation and how drastic of a change you need to make.

4) Cut Household Consumption

Be more aware about lights left on in your house that don't need to be, as well as excess water use (extra-long showers, leaky taps, etc.), and even electronics that are always plugged in and on.

These tips may save you pennies, but in the long run they can really have an impact on your expenses, and you will be thankful that you considered them now.

5) Freebies Are Everywhere!

Freebies really are everywhere; you just have to look for them. There are many websites online that share freebies or have promotional deals for certain small businesses in your area that you can take advantage of.

Some great freebies that I personally like are Kindle eBooks that go on promotion regularly. You can find them through the Kindle Store "Free" section.

Why spend money buying and downloading books when you can just search through and check out what books are free every week.

Also, use your local library, they offer books for free, magazines for free, music for free (usually), and also movies for free!

6) Alternatives to Going Out

Rather than going out for dinner, why not host a night in at your place and ask your friends over? You can host a potluck dinner and each person can bring a dish.

The same goes for movies, instead of going out for movies you can just get movies from the library for free or rent one for $1 (instead of spending upwards of $10+ on movie tickets) from one of those DVD rental boxes in front of stores.

7) Alternatives to Paid Attractions

Instead of going out and spending money on attractions, consider going to a park for free, maybe even having a picnic?

Also, there are many free concerts, festivals and events run locally at community halls, parks and show grounds. You can most likely find them online or in local newspapers.

8) Cut the Coffees & Lunches

If you're in debt and working on ways to reduce your expenses, you definitely shouldn't be spending money on your morning coffee. Instead of buying it, simply have it at home.

The same goes with lunch, instead of buying your lunch every day, pack it at home and take it with you.

9) Prepare When You Shop

Before you go to the store to do your grocery shopping, make sure you create a list and stick to it. There's no need to stray off the list and buy things that aren't on there because it will only lead to extra money being spend on unnecessary things.

Also, try to eat at home before you go shopping. If you're less hungry while at the store you're less likely to buy unnecessary food.

When shopping, choose cheaper alternatives – a lot of the time the cheaper brands can taste the same, if not, better!

10) Cut Out Unnecessary Subscriptions

If you haven't already thought of these, definitely cut out newspaper and magazine subscriptions!

Simply use the Internet, if you still have it at home, or go to the library if you don't, and you can consume the same knowledge online that you can from those newspapers and magazines.

11) Cut Out the Gym Membership

If you're not a regular goer to the gym, cut it out!

And even if you are, but you only do mainly cardio workouts, cut it out anyway! You can do so many amazing cardio workouts outside, from jogging, to sprints, or going to go park and running up hills.

You can also find some stairs and climb them and add that to your workout.

If you live near a beach, go for a run on the sand, or even a swim!

There are many options when you start looking for them!

Remember not all of these tips above will apply to you. I do admit that some are quite extreme, but when you start paying off large amounts of your debt you will be thankful!

You can also start bringing back some of these things eventually once your debt is eliminated or nearing elimination. This doesn't have to be a permanent change.

The truth is, though, using the above methods effectively can save you upwards of hundreds of dollars every single month!

Step 7 – Create A New Financial System

Hopefully you understand everything I've discussed up until now, and that you have already or plan on implementing a lot of it in your life.

Right now, we're going to take a look at creating a completely new system for your finances, which is based off your monthly budget.

Why is a financial system beneficial?

It keeps track of every dollar coming in and going out of your pocket.

It allows you to commit the largest amounts of money to your debts right now, and even if you didn't have debt, it would allow you to commit the largest amounts of money to your investments, hobbies or vacations.

At the end of the day, achieving financial freedom isn't about how much money you make; rather, it's about how much money you keep. And at the most fundamental level, a financial system focuses on keeping more money in your hands after all of your expenses.

Create A Budget

Now that we have assessed our income and expenses on a monthly basis, and we have the ability to increase our income as much as possible, as well as decrease our expenses as much as possible, we can make a somewhat accurate budget that gives us solid estimations of monthly incomes and expenses.

This is exactly what I want you to do. You now have a lot more information than you had previously, so there is no reason why you cannot make a more accurate and reliable budget.

This budget will then be used to estimate future monthly incomes and expenses, and it will be used as the foundation of our financial system.

Remember you don't have to get it right the first time; you can always make changes as the months go on. With the financial system I present below, given a worst possible scenario, there are still funds you can access from your savings account again (debt payments occur after all expenses are incurred).

Emergency Fund

This is a quick interruption to the flow of this current step, but it's something I want to introduce and emphasize the importance of.

An emergency fund is essentially a separate bank account (usually a high interest online account) that holds cash that you have socked away for a "rainy day".

Ideally, we want about $1,000 in our emergency fund, and we only touch is in the case of an emergency.

Why is it important?

The main reason it's important is because it will hopefully be the funds you will use in replacement of your credit card. Usually when there's an emergency and you don't have enough money in your bank account, you'd put the charge on your credit card. This time, however, you will have this emergency fund to fall back on.

Honestly, at this current stage when paying off your debt is your largest priority, it's obvious that you can't just create an emergency fund and put $1,000 into it.

So, what I recommend is that you take 5% of your Wipe Out Money every month and put it to your emergency fund. Once the fund hits $1,000 you can put this 5% back to your Wipe Out Money and contribute it to your debt.

Monthly Financial System

We're going to take a look at this monthly financial system now, and the best way I recommend setting it up for the most benefit from your Wipe Out Money.

For this system to work fully, you need to have two bank accounts, a checking and a savings account. A third account will also be needed for your emergency fund. If you don't already have three accounts, you can contact your bank and get that sorted without any issues.

We are also assuming in this process below that you get paid a paycheck from your employer once a month. If you get paid weekly, biweekly, or inconsistently (from another income source) you can still apply this same process by choosing the same payday that occurs every month. For example, if you get paid every two weeks, simply pick the first payment of the month as your "Day One".

Now that you know this, we can get to the system.

1) Income

As mentioned several chapters ago, this includes all the money coming into your bank account. The money comes into your checking account on your payday (Day One) and that same day or the day after you have an automatic transfer that sends your Wipe Out Money automatically to your savings account.

If you haven't figured it out already, we have to assign the amount of our Wipe Out Money *BEFORE* the month begins to set this up automatically.

This means that after the Wipe Out Money is sent to the savings account, the amount left in the checking account will be exactly what we need to spend on our expenses for the month. This is where the accuracy and good estimation of our monthly expenses comes into play (you can give yourself a little bit of buffer room and overestimate expenses slightly).

This is great for two reasons.

Firstly, you are paying yourself first, and by paying yourself first, you're ensuring your debt gets paid first.

Secondly, you are giving yourself an actual monetary limit. Having X amount of dollars in your account to spend on expenses will ensure you only spend X since you can't go over.

2) Expenses

If allowed, you want to automate as many of your bills as possible and get them set up to automatically deduct the payment from your checking account - this will save you time.

For any bills that can't be done automatically, for example, rent, you can go to an ATM and withdraw the cash for it.

For groceries, you can use a debit card that is attached to your checking account, or again, withdraw the cash out from an ATM.

The point is that your budget for expenses for the month was as accurate as possible so that you don't need to touch any of the Wipe Out Money in your savings!

If anything, hopefully you have some money left over before your next payday, after all expenses are paid. If this is the case, send this extra money also to your savings account, adding it to your Wipe Out Money.

3) Wipe Out Money

So right now, once all expenses are paid, you're left with your Wipe Out Money in your savings account, and that's it!

On the day before your next monthly payday, or two days

prior to your next payday, you want to go through and do the following step.

4) Emergency Fund

Right before your next payday, send 5% of the amount in your savings account to ANOTHER savings account, which will act as your emergency fund account.

Hopefully this other account is a very high interest rate account, gaining you the best interest on the money that sits there.

5) Wipe Out Money (minus 5%) Thrown at Debt

The remaining money in your first savings account will be your Wipe Out Money, and on your next payday (when you see the money in your checking account) send all of this Wipe Out Money to the first debt on your "Debt Sheet"!

The reason we wait until we get the money in our checking account is so that we always have access to money in case we ever need it for anything. Keep in mind that when our emergency fund is also established we will have another buffer of safety.

Now repeat the cycle every month with the new paycheck money. Remember that when your emergency fund has $1,000, you can either keep contributing to it if you want, or just skip that step and throw all your money to your debt.

Step 8 – The Secret to Eliminating Debt FAST

The WOM Avalanche Effect

This is the secret to the system and why it works at eliminating your debt fast!

In the beginning, you are throwing all your extra chunks of money (your Wipe Out Money) at the first debt on your "Debt Sheet". This is crucial and must be done so that you can speed up the process.

Once that first debt is paid off, since the compulsory debt repayments from that debt is now gone, your monthly expenses decrease, meaning you have even MORE Wipe Out Money to throw at your next debt!

So, you will effectively contribute *more money* every month to that second debt, paying it off at a faster rate!

Once that is paid off, your expenses decrease even more and your Wipe Out Money gets even bigger for your next debts!

Your next debt is also paid off at an even faster rate.

This will continue and your Wipe Out Money will grow at an exponential rate, meaning that you are contributing exponentially greater chunks of money to your debts.

Now, if you have only one big debt, this is the same thing.

Every time you throw massive chunks of money at your one big debt, it's reducing the compulsory repayments every month, decreasing your monthly expenses, and increasing your Wipe Out Money!

This keeps going on and on in the same cycle that it would if the debts were separate.

I'm sure that now you can see why this system it not only better than other debt repayment systems, but it also leads to one of the fastest methods of paying off debt.

Other systems may allow you to adjust your expenses and make them larger once you start paying off parts of your debt, however, with my system I encourage that you maintain the same budget throughout, and if anything you try to keep increasing your Wipe Out Money until the last cent of debt is paid off. This is the key, and is the secret that leads to exponential repayments and fast elimination of your debt.

Accelerate Your Debt Repayments Even More

Above I showed you that by keeping your income and fixed expenses the same, as soon as you start paying off debt your expenses decrease, so your Wipe Out Money increases.

What if you start implementing some of those tips that I gave you about increasing your income?

If you get a second job or do some work on the side and increase your income, then your Wipe Out Money gets even bigger!

What if you *also* start implementing some of the tips I gave you to help reduce your expenses?

Then your Wipe Out Money will get *EVEN BIGGER!*

As you can see, this system allows for serious acceleration of your debt repayments. The main reason is because it requires discipline and focuses on what needs to be done – paying the debt.

While the emergency debt is growing (keep in mind that if the Wipe Out Money keeps getting bigger, then the 5% contributions to the emergency fund also keep getting bigger), it will eventually hit the $1,000 mark. At this point you can stop doing the 5% transfers to the emergency fund.

Guess what?

That's even MORE money to throw at your debt!

Step 9 – Debts Paid, Now What?

Before you know it, if you stick to the system, your debts will be paid off!

You will also have learned how to effectively follow a budget and create and follow a successful financial system.

The first thing I want to advise you is to avoid debt as much as you can, the last thing you want it is to end up in the same spot again.

Secondly, and most importantly, embrace your awesome financial education that you would have developed and learned over this journey.

You have created a system that successfully works and if you maintain it you can use the assigned Wipe Out Money (once you have no debt) to fund your passions, dreams and hobbies!

I am currently working on another book discussing how to structure a sound financial system when you have no major debts so you can achieve your dreams.

Here's a brief run down.

Focus on splitting your Wipe Out Money into things like holiday accounts, hobby accounts, retirement accounts, children college accounts, etc.

The point is that you're not just spending recklessly; instead, you're keeping track of your money still.

You can definitely give yourself more room for expenses (and get all those nice things back in your life!), but you still want some control because without it you may end up back in debt, or without savings.

Conclusion

I'd like to congratulate you for getting to the end of this book and understanding my system.

Even though this system is effective and works, it does require effort and discipline. And I can promise you one thing; if you don't put in the work and take action, you won't get anywhere.

I have given you the steps, and I hope you can use it and change your life for the better!

Please remember it's possible and you can achieve financial freedom. Just believe and take appropriate action.

Don't forget to grab my 100% FREE Bonus Guide - $1k/M: How to Make an Extra $1,000/Month Online!

This guide will help you increase your income, starting TODAY!

Final Words

I would like to thank you for downloading my book and I hope I have been able to help you and educate you about something new.

If you have enjoyed this book and would like to share your positive thoughts, could you please take 30 seconds of your time to go back and give me a review on my Amazon book page!

I greatly appreciate seeing these reviews because it helps me share my hard work!

Again, thank you and I wish you all the best with your endeavors!

PS: Don't forget you can contact me via my blog at http://www.thebigventure.com

Other Books By Ashton Jude

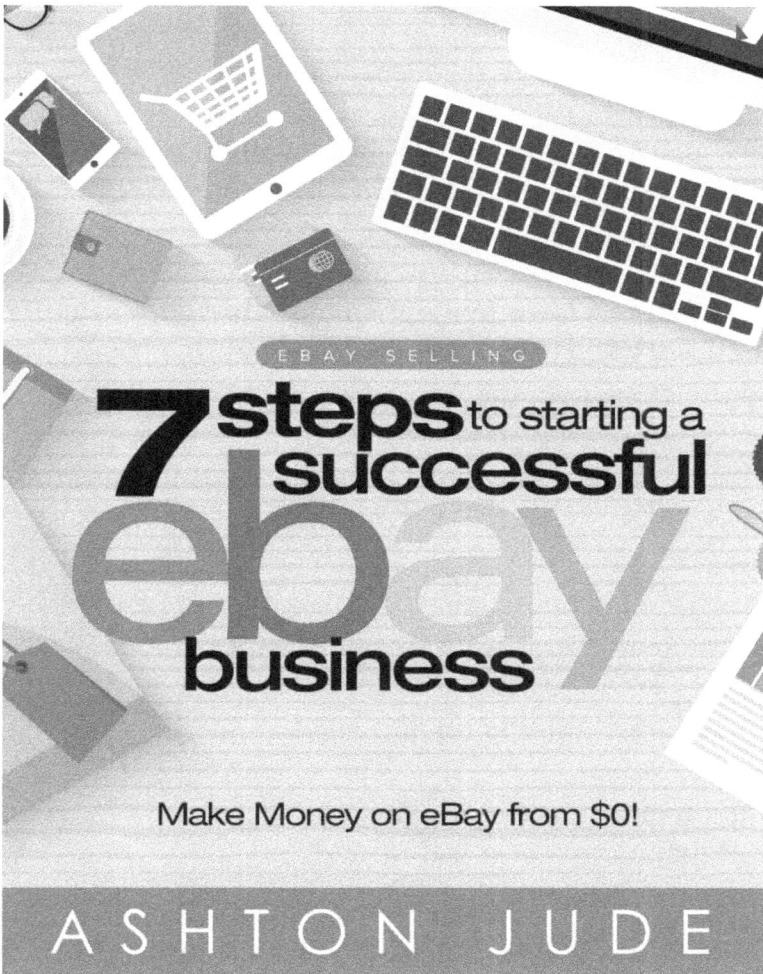

Check out: 7 Steps to Starting a Successful eBay Business

Disclaimer

I have created this eBook with the purpose to provide information on paying debt and the money management.

It is sold with the understanding that the author and publisher are not engaged in any sort of professional services or legal advice.

Every effort has been made to ensure this book is complete and without error, however, it's possible that there may be errors, whether in content or other.

Therefore, do not consider this to be anything more than a guide and a book created for entertainment purposes.

The author and publisher are not liable or responsible for any damages or losses incurred by any person, which has allegedly been caused directly or indirectly by the information within this book.

If you do not agree with the above information, simply contact the author for a full refund.

www.ingramcontent.com/pod-product-compliance
Lightning Source LLC
Chambersburg PA
CBHW030535210326
41597CB00014B/1151